Street by Street

CHELMSFORD
BRAINTREE, MALDON, WITHAM

Boreham, Coggeshall, Danbury, East Hanningfield, Galleywood, Great Baddow, Great Notley, Hatfield Peverel, Ingatestone, Kelvedon, Writtle

C000064178

2nd edition July 2006
© Automobile Association Developments Limited 2006

Original edition printed September 2002

Ordnance Survey® This product includes map data licensed from Ordnance Survey® with the permission of the Controller of Her Majesty's Stationery Office. © Crown copyright 2006. All rights reserved. Licence number 399221.

Published by AA Publishing (a trading name of Automobile Association Developments Limited, whose registered office is Fanum House, Basing View, Basingstoke, Hampshire RG21 4EA. Registered number 1878835).

Mapping produced by the Cartography Department of The Automobile Association. (A02660)

A CIP Catalogue record for this book is available from the British Library.

Printed by Oriental Press in Dubai

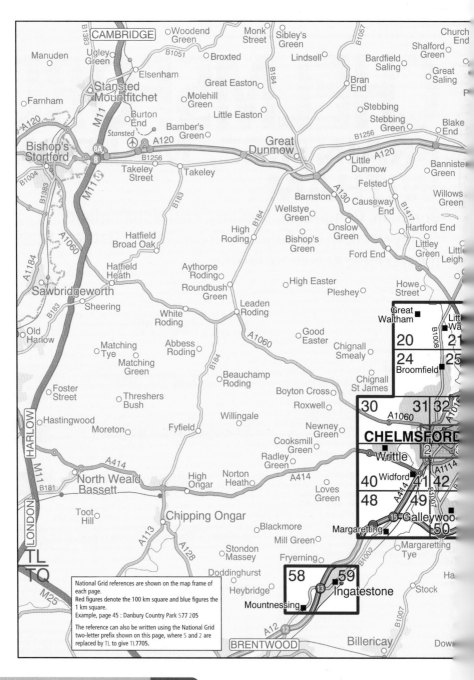

CAMBRIDGE

Manuden
Ugley Green
Elsenham
Stansted Mountfitchet
Farnham
Burton End
Bamber's Green
Bishop's Stortford
Takeley Street
Takeley
Sawbridgeworth
Hatfield Broad Oak
Hatfield Heath
Sheering
White Roding
Old Harlow
Matching Tye
Abbess Roding
Matching Green
Foster Street
Threshers Bush
Hastingwood
Moreton
Fyfield
North Weald Bassett
Toot Hill
Chipping Ongar
High Ongar
Norton Heath

Woodend Green
Broxted
Molehill Green
Little Easton
Great Easton
Bambers Green
Great Dunmow
High Roding
Aythorpe Roding
Roundbush Green
Leaden Roding
Beauchamp Roding
Willingale
Boyton Cross
Roxwell
Newney Green
Cooksmill Green
Radley Green
Loves Green

Monk Street
Sibley's Green
Lindsell
Bran End
Stebbing
Stebbing Green
Little Dunmow
Felsted
Barnston
Wellstye Green
Bishop's Green
Onslow Green
Ford End
High Easter
Pleshey
Good Easter
Chignall Smealy
Chignall St James

Church End
Shalford Green
Great Saling
Bardfield Saling
Blake End
Bannister Green
Willows Green
Hartford End
Littley Green
Little Leigh
Causeway End
Howe Street

Great Waltham
Little Wa
20 Litt Wa **21**
24 **25** Broomfield
30 **31** **32**
CHELMSFORD
Writtle
40 Widford **41** **42**
48 **49**
Galleywoo
50
Margaretting
Margaretting Tye

58 **59**
Ingatestone
Heybridge
Mountnessing
Blackmore
Mill Green
Stondon Massey
Fryerning
Doddinghurst

Stock
Ha

TL
TQ

BRENTWOOD
Billericay
Dow

National Grid references are shown on the map frame of each page.
Red figures denote the 100 km square and blue figures the 1 km square.
Example, page 45 : Danbury Country Park 577 205

The reference can also be written using the National Grid two-letter prefix shown on this page, where 5 and 2 are replaced by TL to give TL7705.

Enlarged scale pages **1:10,000** 6.3 inches to 1 mile

0   1/4   miles   1/2
0   1/4   1/2   kilometres   3/4   1

SUDBURY

IPSWICH

Rose Green

Chappel

Fordstreet

West Bergholt

High Garrett

Burton's Green

Eight Ash Green

A1124

Colchester

5

Stisted

Great Tey

Aldham

Pattiswick Green

26

Beacon End

Stanway

8 9

Braintree

A120

10 11

Coggeshall

Little Tey

A120

Marks Tey

B1408

Copford Green

Easthorpe

Heckfordbridge

Black Notley

Cressing

Silver End

Hardy's Green

Layer de la Haye

Hawbush Green

Feering

Kelvedon

Smythe's Green

Birch

Birch Green

Abberton

The Green

White Notley

14 15

Messing

Layer Marney

Layer Breton

Peldon

Fairstead

16 17

Chipping Hill

Witham

22

Tiptree Heath

Tiptree

Little Braxted

Great Braxted

Oxley Green

Tolleshunt Knights

Great Wigborough

Salcott-cum-Virley

18 19

22 23

Great Totham

West Mersea

Hatfield Peverel

Wickham Bishops

Great Totham

Tolleshunt D'Arcy

Tolleshunt Major

Tollesbury

28 29

Langford

Heybridge

Goldhanger

Bradwell Waterside

35 36 37

Little Baddow

Woodham Walter

38 39

Maldon

Northey Island

Osea Island

River Blackwater

St Lawrence Bay

Ramsey Island

45 46 47

Danbury

Woodham Mortimer

A414

St Lawrence

Tillingham

54 55

Cock Clarks

Rudley Green

Mundon Hill

Steeple

Dengie

53

Purleigh

Maylandsea

Mayland

Asheldham

Howegreen

Latchingdon

Southminster

TL / TQ

57

Woodham Ferrers

Stow Maries

Cold Norton

B1010

Althorne

Rettendon

South Woodham Ferrers

North Fambridge

Bridgemarsh Island

Burnham-on-Crouch

Hullbridge

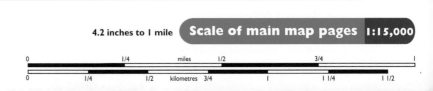

Junction 9	Motorway & junction
Services	Motorway service area
	Primary road single/dual carriageway
Services	Primary road service area
	A road single/dual carriageway
	B road single/dual carriageway
	Other road single/dual carriageway
	Minor/private road, access may be restricted
← ←	One-way street
	Pedestrian area
	Track or footpath
	Road under construction
	Road tunnel
P	Parking
P+	Park & Ride
	Bus/coach station
	Railway & main railway station
	Railway & minor railway station
⊖	Underground station
⊖	Light railway & station
+++++++++	Preserved private railway

LC	Level crossing
•—•—•—•	Tramway
- - - - - -	Ferry route
....	Airport runway
— · — · —	County, administrative boundary
▼▼▼▼▼▼▼	Mounds
17	Page continuation 1:15,000
3	Page continuation to enlarged scale 1:10,000
	River/canal, lake, pier
	Aqueduct, lock, weir
465 ▲ Winter Hill	Peak (with height in metres)
	Beach
	Woodland
	Park
	Cemetery
	Built-up area
	Industrial/business building
	Leisure building
	Retail building
	Other building

⊓⊔⊓⊔⊓⊔	City wall	⚔	Castle
A&E	Hospital with 24-hour A&E department	🏛	Historic house or building
PO	Post Office	Wakehurst Place NT	National Trust property
📖	Public library	🏛	Museum or art gallery
i	Tourist Information Centre	🐎	Roman antiquity
i	Seasonal Tourist Information Centre	⬛	Ancient site, battlefield or monument
⛽⛽	Petrol station, 24 hour Major suppliers only	▦	Industrial interest
✝	Church/chapel	❀	Garden
🚻	Public toilets	◉	Garden Centre Garden Centre Association Member
♿	Toilet with disabled facilities	🌳	Garden Centre Wyevale Garden Centre
PH	Public house AA recommended	🌲	Arboretum
🍴	Restaurant AA inspected	🛒	Farm or animal centre
Madeira Hotel	Hotel AA inspected	🦌	Zoological or wildlife collection
🎭	Theatre or performing arts centre	🦜	Bird collection
👥	Cinema	🦆	Nature reserve
⚑	Golf course	🐟	Aquarium
▲	Camping AA inspected	V	Visitor or heritage centre
🚐	Caravan site AA inspected	⍦	Country park
▲🚐	Camping & caravan site AA inspected	⌒	Cave
🎢	Theme park	🛠	Windmill
🏛	Abbey, cathedral or priory	🛢	Distillery, brewery or vineyard

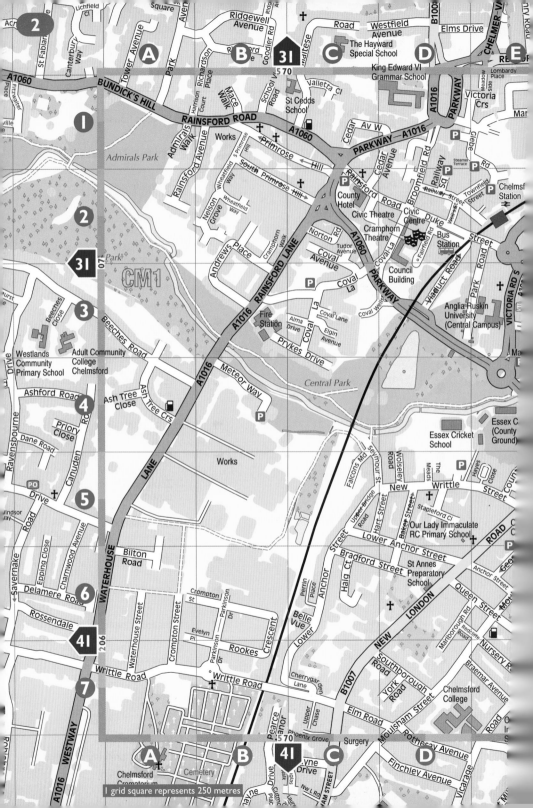

Garrett

Sunnyfields Road

Trotters' Rest

E **F** **G** **H**

77 78

I

GARRETT

HIGH

Grove Field

Grove Orch

A131

BROAD ROAD

26

Willoughby's Lane

Willoughby's Farm

2

Woolmer Farm

Lyons Hall Road

Lyons Hall

3

Thistley Green Road

A131

25

Thistley Green Road

ROAD

Highfield Stile Farm

4

Works

River Blackwater

5

A131

Collingwood Close

Hereford Dr

Hereford

Bridport

Albemarle Gdns

Cavendish Gdns

Vernon Way

Sheene Grove

Nptn Cl

Nptn Cl

Brdpt Ann

Brchr

224

Jenkin's F

Mountbatten

Blake Dr

Gilbert Way

Road

Rayleigh Close

77 78

Fawen Gdns

Wy

Wyng Gdns

Fisher Wy

Keble

Stafford Crs

Par Cl

E **F** **8** **G** **H**

V C

Alax Close

Achille

SVC

Trafalgar Way

Edinburgh

Wellington Close

Beatty Gdns

Fisher Wy

Dr Gdn

Lyons Hall County Prim School

Feign Cl

Crown Meadow

Deerleap Wy

Dunoon

naught Gardens

Hawkins Way

Dr Gdn

Kings Lane

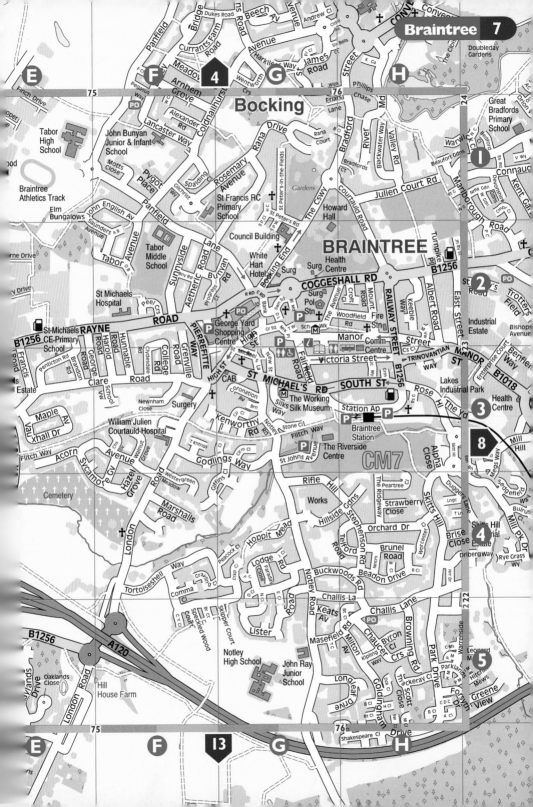

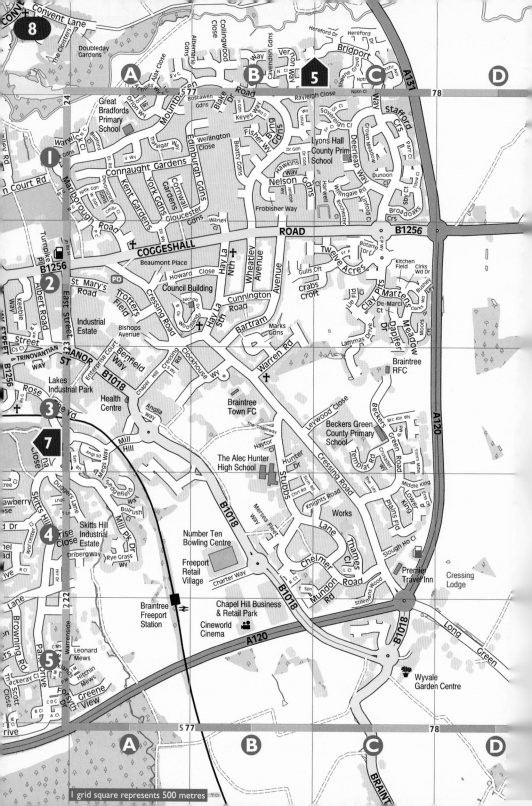

10

A   B   C   D

5 83   84

24   Hovells Farm

Cradle House

1

2   Holfield Grange

23

Am

3   Road   Coggeshall Road   COGGESHALL ROAD   A120

Highfields

West Street

Grigg's Farm   Coggeshall Town FC

4   River Blackwater

Essex Way

22

Essex Way

5   Curd Hall Farm

Essex Way

A   B   C   D

5 83   84

Herons Farm

Cuthedge Lane

Brook

1 grid square represents 500 metres

E F G H

85 86 24

Hall

Road

ROAD

Bouchi
Grang

Farm

I

A120

B1024

Tilkey

Monk Downs
Farm

Tey Road

Industrial
Estate

The
Honeywood
School

Colne

Prior's
Way

Essex Way

2

St
Nicholas
WY

Westfield
Dr

Honeywood Avenue

Gurton

The Bramleys

Fabians Rd

Paycocke Way

Monkdowns
Road

Wisdoms
Green

Tey Road

Brick
Kiln
Cl

Fabians
Road

23

Damaskes
Road

Hitcham Rd

Hawkes Rd

Les Rd

Buxton Road

Windmill
Fields

The
Greenways

Churchfield
Road

Jaggard's Road

Cemetery

†

Church
Green

†

St Peter's Road

Essex Way

Tilkey Road

Vesta
Close

Robinsbridge

Stoneham St

Walford
Way

G RW

Vane La

Nunns
Close

St Peters
CE Primary
School

MV71
Rd

Mounts
Rd

Hill Road

3

all

Knights Acre
Road

Surgery

†

Queen Street

Albert
Place

†

Swan Street

Albert
Gardens

St
Annes
Close

parklands

COLCHESTER ROAD

Colchester
Road

COLCHE

Kings

H

Church Street

B1024

White Hart
Hotel

Market End

20 MPH

PO

The
Gravel

Lakes
Meadow

aycocke's
ouse (NT)

Greenacres

Barn View
Road

Abbey

Lane

†

Essex Way

Coggeshall Road (Feering)

4

Grange
Barn (NT)

Essex Way

22

Grange Farm

5

Feeringbury

B1024

**Coggeshall
Hamlet**

Pointwell

E F G H

85 86

Scrip's

Old Mill
Lane

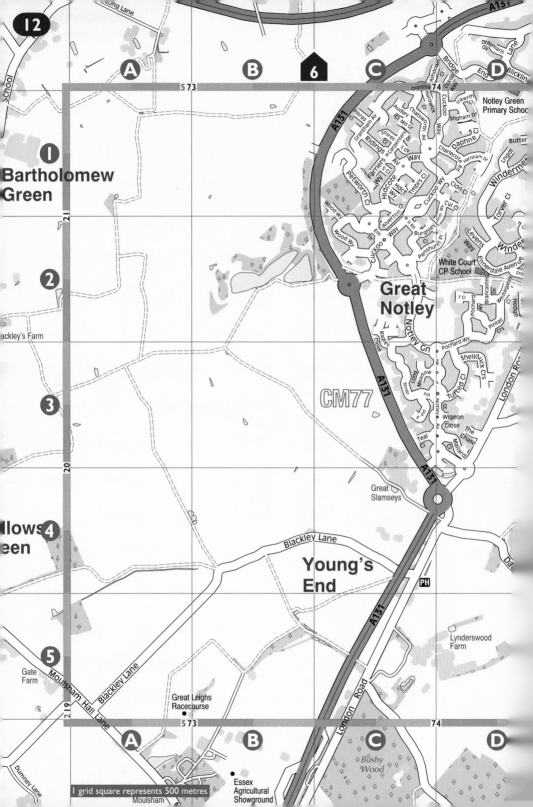

I2

Young Lane

School

A131

Blicklin

Draymans Ov

Lane

Bridge End

cranthai

Notley Green Primary Schoo

1

Bartholomew Green

Ribrop

Crantham Av

Audley

Chatswo rth

Hartwick

Cuckoo Way

Mo Cr

Ickwrth Cl

Shgham Dr

Butter

Shires

Carpenters Dr

Daphne Cl

Ridings

CV

Charlecote

lngdl

Winderme

Farriers

Wy

Hilcote

Wy

HdCt

Tmbrs Cl

Cldn Cl

ra Harnham dr

Torver Cl

Petworth Cl

Cuckoo Wy

CVI Cl

Wdr

Winde

Wood Wy

Em

Alverton Cl

H Rd

Ffrm Wy

Levens Way

Ennerdale Avenue

Wood Wy

Cuckoo Way

Burgnley Pl

Penshurst Cl

White Court C.P. School

2

ckley's Farm

Great Notley

Ragley Close

Pochard Wy

Brancaster

Wyntegarden

Hedge

3

CM77

Notley Gn

Pochard Wy

Shellduck Crs

Pintail Crs

London Ro

Long Meadow Fld

Strmr

Tufted Cl

The Chase

Wigeon Close

Notley Av

E Fld

Teal Cl

Mallard

4 llows
een

Great Slamseys

Blackley Lane

Young's End

PH

A131

5

Gate Farm

Moulsham Hall Lane

Blackley Lane

Lynderswood Farm

Great Leighs Racecourse

London Road

A131

Dumney Lane

Bushy Wood

Essex Agricultural Showground

Moulsham

I grid square represents 500 metres

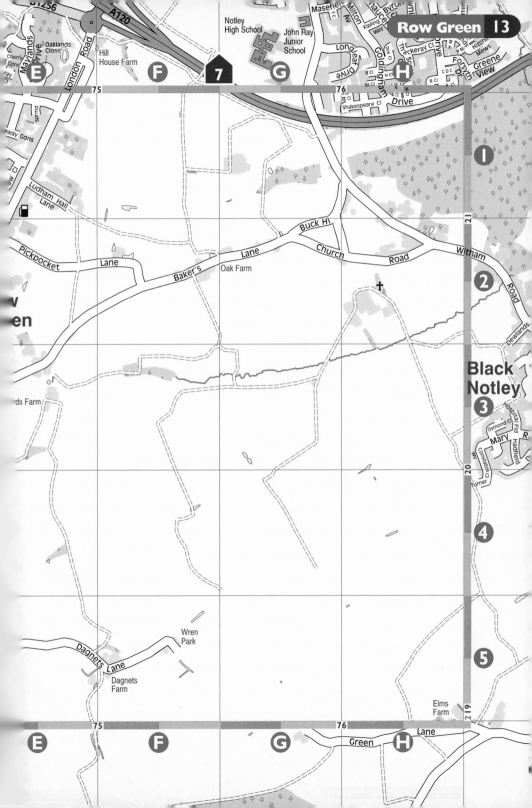

BT256

A120

Maylands Drive

Oaklands Close

London Road

Hill House Farm

E

F

7

Notley High School

John Ray Junior School

G

Masefiel

Milton

Byron

Kipling Way

Long leaf Drive

Goldingham Drive

Thackeray Drive

Hitchin Mews

Forsyth

Greene View

H

Shakespeare Cl

Drive

75

76

Cherry

way Gdns

Sprgs

I

Ludham Hall Lane

Pickpocket Lane

Baker's Lane

Oak Farm

Buck Hi Lane

Church Road

Witham

Dewlands

2

21

Black Notley

3

ds Farm

Osmond Cl

Hospital Fld

Mary

Constable Cl

Turner

Hadfield

R

W

4

20

5

Dagnets Lane

Wren Park

Dagnets Farm

Elms Farm

219

75

76

Green

Lane

E

F

G

H

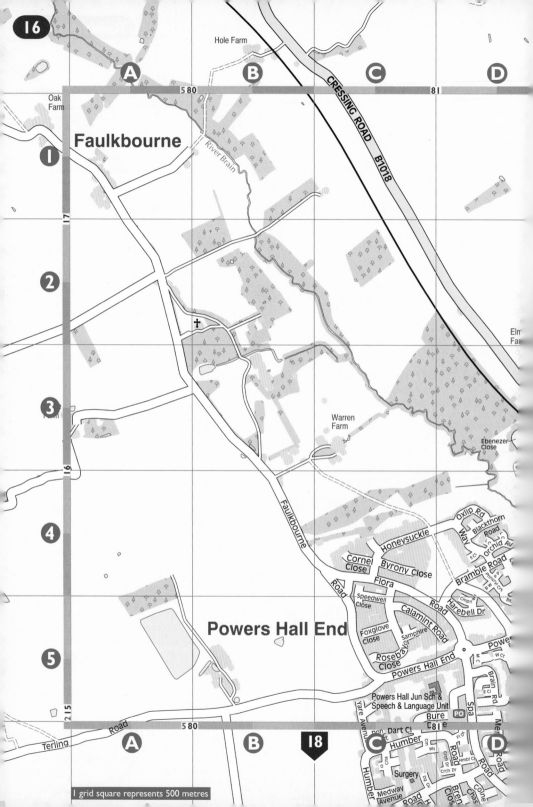

Hole Farm

CRESSING ROAD

B1018

A 580 **B** **C** 81 **D**

Oak Farm

Faulkbourne

River Brain

17

1

2

16

†

3

Warren Farm

Ebenezer Close

Elm Fa

4

Faulkbourne Road

Oxlip Rd

Blackthorn Road

Honeysuckle Way

Orchid Av

Cornel Close

Byrony Close

Bramble Road

Flora

Harebell Dr

Speedwell Close

Calamint Road

Powers Hall End

Foxglove Close

Samphire

Rosebay Close

Powers Hall End

Powe

Brain Rd

5

Powers Hall Jun Sch & Speech & Language Unit

Yare Avenue

PO

Bure

Spa

2 15

A 580 **B** **C** Humber **D**

Terling Road

Dart Cl

Surgery

Humber

Medway Avenue

Road

Mel Road

81

Colne Clos

Bren

I grid square represents 500 metres

E   F   G   H

82   83

Rivenhall CE
Primary School

PO

St Mary's
Rd

Tusser Close
Beech Road

Hoo Hall

Tarecroft
Wood

Rivenhall

Stovern's Hall

Oak Road

I

17

2

Rickstones Road

Rectory Lane

Golf Course

16

3

uthview
ool

Elm Hall County
Primary School

stones
Road

Road

Blake Campbell Rd

Virgil Road

Shaw Road

Bronte Road

Templars County
J&I School

Cross Road

ROAD

Forest Road

Drive

Chrr Rd

Cedar

Elm Rise

Dorothy Drive

Willow Rise

Rowan Way

Laburnum Way

Mott Cl

Poplar Close

Lime Cl

New Close

Juniper Crs

CM8

Rivenhall
Oaks Golf
Club

St Nicholas
Close

St Nicholas Road

Street

Manor Rd

Witham
Cemetery

Cypress Road

Homefield Rd

Walnut Drive

Chalks Road

BRAINTREE ROAD

Superstore

Throat

Cut

LC

Motts Lane

LC

Eastways Lane

Works

Waterside
Business
Park

J22

4

215

5

Coleman's
Farm

ing Hill

Moat Farm

Chipping Hill

Chase Lane

White Horse Lane

Braintree Road

Albert Rd

Easton Road

Station Rd

Croft Way

Croft Way

Eastways

Bellcroft

Crittall Road

COLCHESTER ROAD B1389

Freebournes Road

Works

Little Braxted Lane

Witham Station

Janmead

Avenue Road

ROAD

Moss Road

Stepfield

82   83

E   F   **19**   G   H

Surgery

COLLINGWOOD ROAD

The Paddocks

Whitehall Ct

CAB

War
Mem

Pol
Stn

NEWLAND STREET

Mag
Ct

Abercorn Way

Health

The Grove

Works

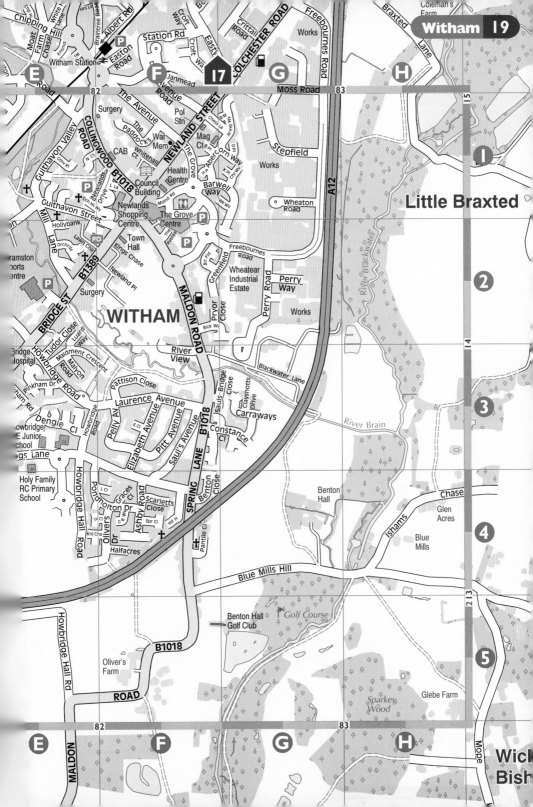

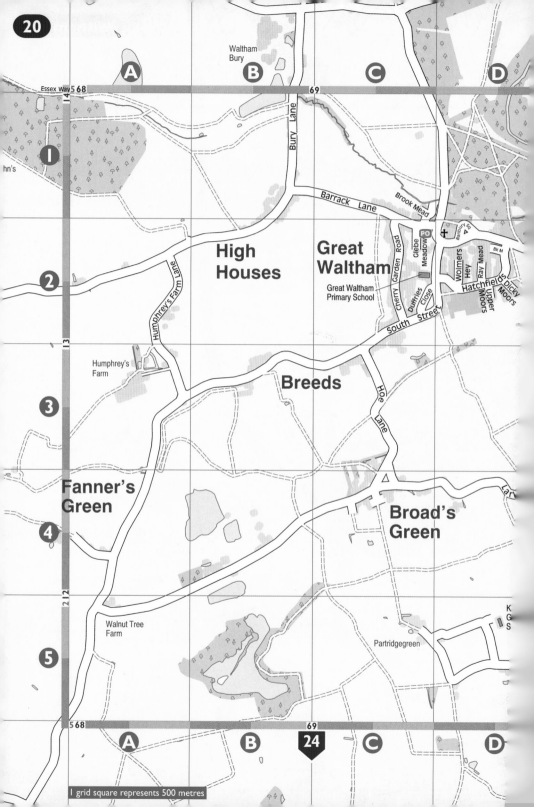

A Waltham Bury B C D

14 68 Essex Way 5 69

hn's

I

Bury Lane

Barrack Lane

Brook Mead

High Houses

Great Waltham

PO

Glebe Meadow

Cherry Garden Road

Banbury Rd

Wolmers Hey

Ray Mead

Bk M

Hatchfields

Dicky Moors

Upper Moors

2

Humphrey's Farm Lane

Great Waltham Primary School

Dunfries Close

South Street

13

3

Humphrey's Farm

Breeds

Hoe Lane

Fanner's Green

4

Broad's Green

La

212

Walnut Tree Farm

K
G
S

5

Partridgegreen

5 68 69

A B 24 C D

E F G H
75 76

Wallace's
Road

Waltham Road

Industrial
Estate

I

Chantry

Waltham Road

2

Porter's
Park

Boreham
Industrial Est

Boleyn Way

MAIN ROAD

B1137

3

A12

Brick
Lane

House
Road

Yonge
Close

H Rd

Dudley
Close

St Andrews Road

Allens Close

Plantation Road

Villiers
Place

Elm Way

Seabrook
Gardens

Claypits
Road

ct

Sussex Close

Haselfoot
Road

Butterfield
Road

Holmans

Hutton Cl

Boons

Falkland
Close

Fitzwalter
Road

Boreham
Primary
School

4

Old Forge
Road

Church Road

Juniper Road

MAIN ROAD

A12

B1137

Premier
Travel Inn

Tyssen
Mead

Lewitt
Place

PO

The
Willows

Surgery

Boreham

The
Chase

Lodge
Crs

The Chase

Old Hall

5

Church Road

J19

E F G H
75 34 76

Boreham
Hall

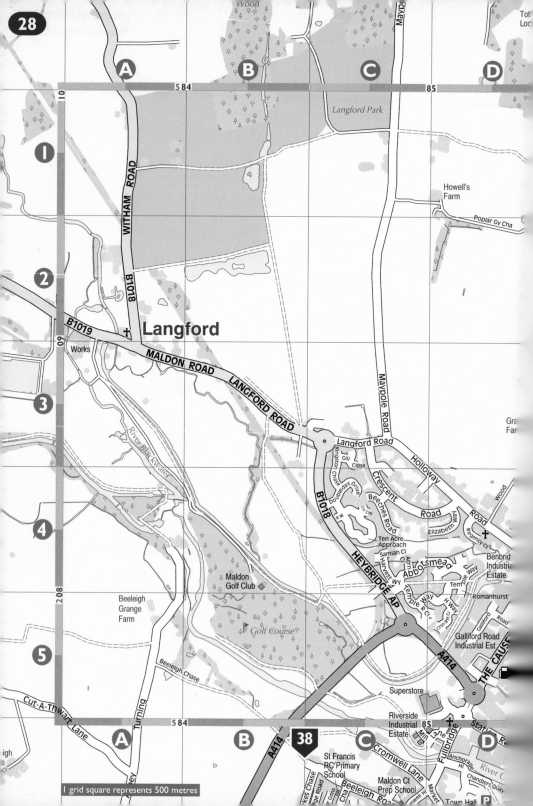

A **B** **C** **D**

584 · · · 85

10

I

WITHAM ROAD

Langford Park

Howell's
Farm

Poplar Gv Cha

2

B1018

B1019

60

Langford

Works

MALDON ROAD

LANGFORD ROAD

River Blackwater

Maypole Road

3

Langford Road

Holloway

Kingston Chase
Gill
Close

Crescent

Road

Road

Wood

4

B1018

Doubleday Drive

Beeches Road

Elizabeth

Regency Ct

Ten Acre
Approach

Samian Cl

Harvest
Wy

Abbotsmead

Benbrid
Industria
Estate

Maldon
Golf Club

HEYBRIDGE AP

Arm
Temple
Way

Temple Rd Cl

Crescent Cl

Romanhurst

Galliford
Road

208

Beeleigh
Grange
Farm

Galliford Road
Industrial Est

Golf Course

A414

THE CAUSE

5

Beeleigh Chase

Superstore

Cut-A-Thwart Lane

Turning

Station R

584

A **B** **C** **D**

A414

38

St Francis
RC/Primary
School

Cromwell Lane

Fullbridge

The
Mill

Riverside
Industrial
Estate

Anchorage
Hl

Chandlers Quay

Maldon Ct
Prep School

Beeleigh Road

Market

Town Hall

River C

P

1 grid square represents 500 metres

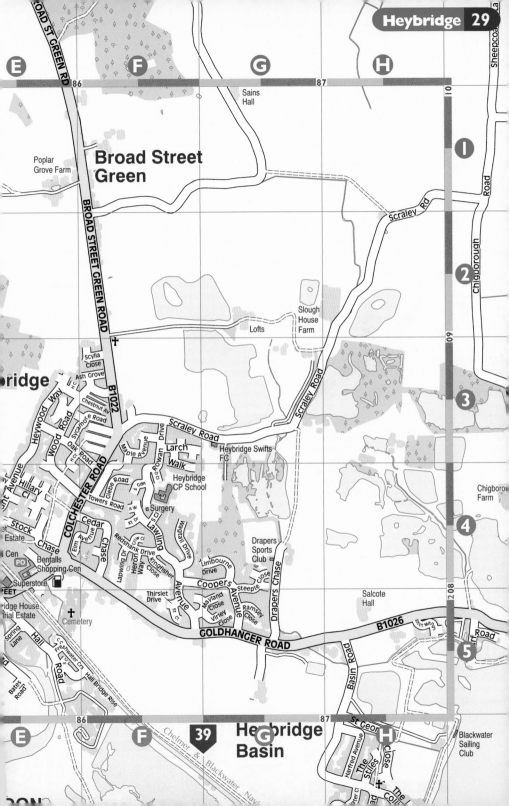

E   F   G   H

86   87   10

Sains Hall

I

Poplar Grove Farm

Broad Street Green

Scraley Rd

BROAD STREET GREEN ROAD

Chigborough Road

2

09

Slough House Farm

Lofts

Scylla Close

Ash Grove

ridge

Chestnut Av

Scraley Road

Heywood Way

Wood Road

Sycamore

Maple Avenue

Rowan Drive

Larch Walk

Heybridge Swifts FC

3

Chigborough Farm

COLCHESTER ROAD

B1022

Oak Road

Glebe Road

Heybridge CP School

Towers Road

Surgery

Hillary Cl

Cedar Avenue

Elm Ave

Chase

Redshank Drive

Lapwing Dr

Heron Way

Kingfisher Close

Wagtail Drive

Limbourne Drive

Drapers Sports Club

Drapers Chase

4

208

stock Estate

Cen

PO

Bentalls Shopping Cen

Superstore

EET

Coopers Avenue

Thirslet Drive

Mayland Close

Virley Close

Ramsey Close

steeple Close

Salcote Hall

ridge House trial Estate

Cemetery

Spring Lane

Freshwater Crs

Hall Road

Bates Road

Hall Bridge Rise

GOLDHANGER ROAD

Basin Road

B1026

Turf Road

5

E   F   G   H

86   87

39

Chelmer & Blackwater Navi

He bridge Basin

St Geor

Harfred Avenue

Close

The Stiles

Blackwater Sailing Club

ON

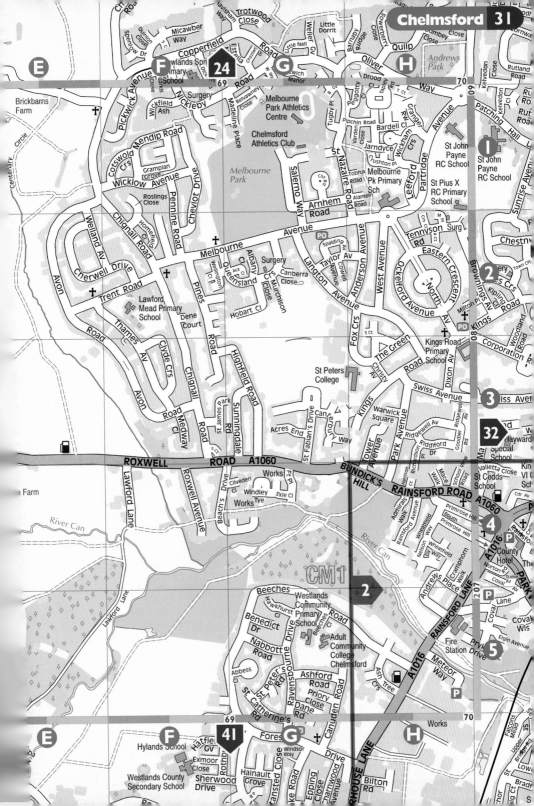

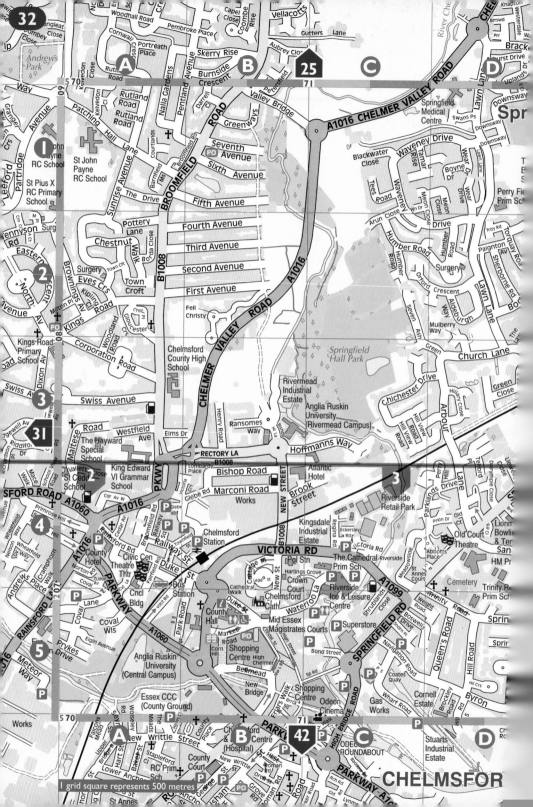

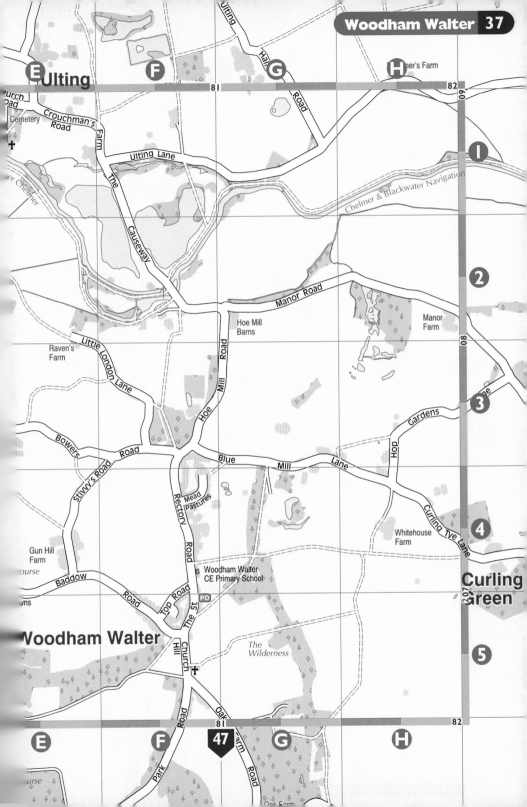

E   F   G   H

Ulting

ner's Farm

81   82

60

Church Road

Cemetery

Crouchman's Road

Ulting Lane

The Farm

Causeway

er Chelmer

Chelmer & Blackwater Navigation

I

2

Manor Road

Manor Farm

80

Hoe Mill Barns

Raven's Farm

Little London Lane

Hoe Mill Road

Gardens

3

Bowers Road

Blue Mill Lane

Hop

Curling Tye Lane

4

Stivvy's Road

Rectory Road

Mead Pastures

Whitehouse Farm

Curling Green

Gun Hill Farm

Woodham Walter CE Primary School

PO

A207

ourse

Baddow Road

Top Road

The St

Woodham Walter

Church Hill

The Wilderness

5

Park

Oak Farm Road

E   F   G   H

81   82

47

E F 31 G H P

Abbess
Nabbott Road
Adult Community College Chelmsford
A1016
Meteor Way
WIS

St Peter's Rd
St Catherine's Rd
Ashford Road
Priory Close
Canuden Road
Ash Tree Crs

Dean Way
Forest
PO
Dane Rd
Works
Falcon's Mead
Upper Bradford St
Lower
Seymour St
Hart St
St A Prep

Hatfield GV
Rothbury Road
Windsor Way
Drive
Bilton Rd
Anchor St
Haig Ct
Bradford

Hylands School
Exmoor Close
Hainault Grove
Stansted Close
Savernake Road
Epping Close
Charnwood Avenue
Delamere Road
Rossendale
WATERHOUSE LANE
Bilton Rd
2
Crompton Street
Crompton St
Evelyn Pl
Rookes Crs
Cherry Gdn La
Writtle Rd
Upper
Elm Road
NEW

Westlands County Secondary School
Sherwood Drive
Milburn Crs
Harewood Road
Waterhouse Street
I

Chelmsford Road
Longacre
Writtle Road
WESTWAY
A1016
Parkinson Dr

Surgery
MOULSHAM STREET

Hanbury Road
Robjohns
Chelmsford Crematorium
Cemetery
Pierce Manor
2
Laurel Grove
Brookland
M

Centenary Circle
Shakestones
Russell Way
Widford Industrial Estate
Farrow Road
Rodney Way
Tattersall Way
Redmayne Drive
Mead Path
LONDON ROAD
Wd Ct
A1114
Widford Chase
Preparatory School
Widford Grove
Road
Wood St
3
Superstore
Bruce Grove
42
Stewart Road
Hillside
WOOD STREET

Megabowl
Widford
Links Drive
Links Drive
Chelmsford Golf Club
St John's Hospital
4
A1007
Surgery
Moulsham Thrift

Hylands Park

Hylands House & Park
Elm Farm
London Road A414
Golf Course
Thrift Farm
5

69 70
E F 49 G H
204

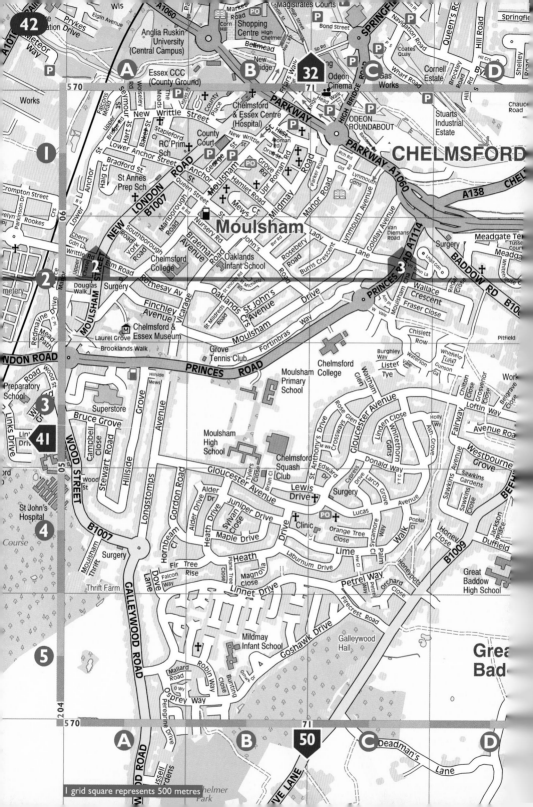

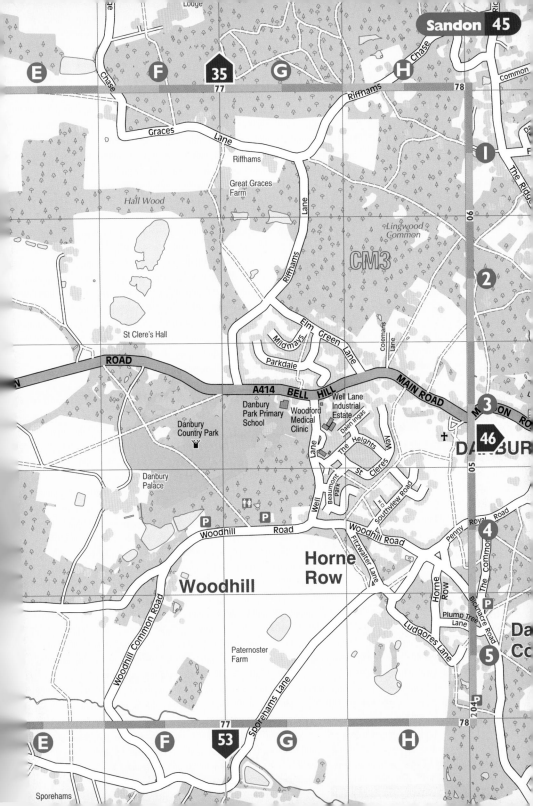

E F **35** G H
77

Chase

Riffhams

Graces Lane

Riffhams

Great Graces Farm

Hall Wood

St Clere's Hall

Lingwood Common

CM3

I

90

2

Elm Green Lane

Mildmays

Parkdale

Colemans Lane

ROAD

A414 BELL HILL

MAIN ROAD

Well Lane Industrial Estate

Danbury Park Primary School

Woodford Medical Clinic

Daen Ingas

Danbury Country Park

The Heights

St Cleres

3

46

DANBUR

Danbury Palace

Well

Beaumont Park

Southview Road

Penny Royal Road

The Common

4

P P

Woodhill Road

Woodhill Road

Fitzwalter Lane

Horne Row

Woodhill

Horne Row

Plump Tree Lane

Bicknacre Road

P

Woodhill Common Road

Paternoster Farm

Ludgores Lane

Da
Co

5

204

Sporehams Lane

E F **53** G H
77

Sporehams

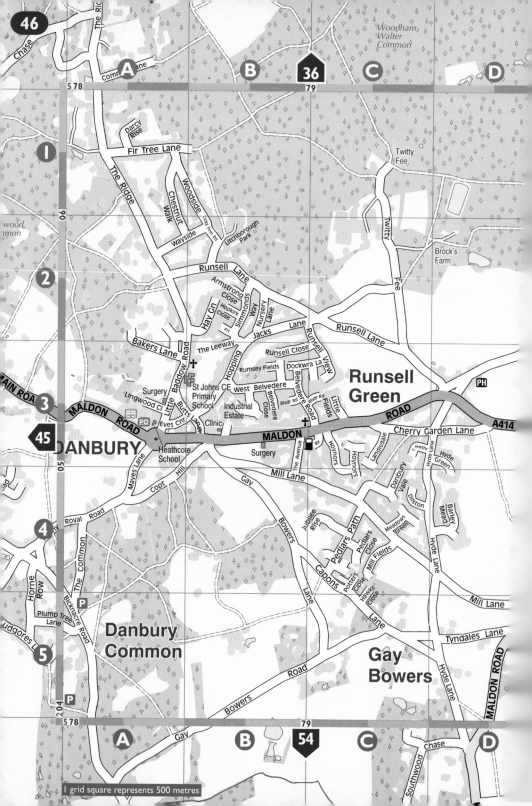

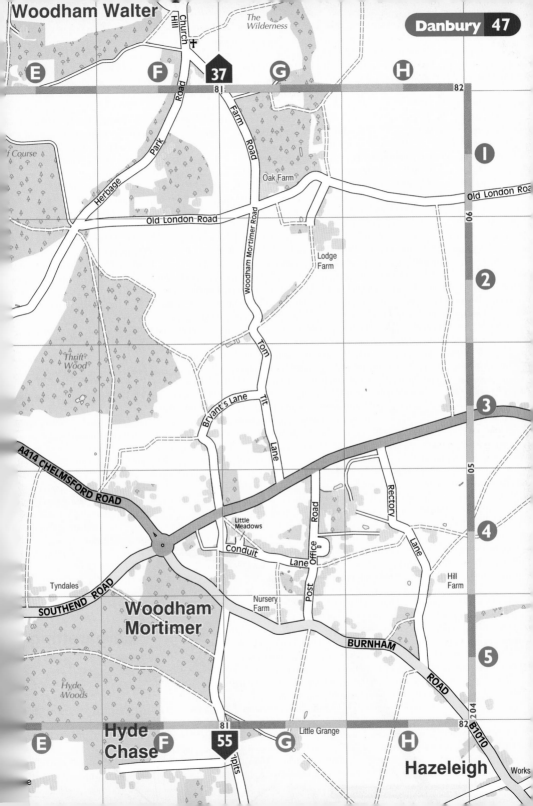

Woodham Walter

The Wilderness

E F 37 G H

81 82

I

Church Hill Road

Park

Herbage

f Course

Farm Road

Oak Farm

Old London Road

Old London Road

Woodham Mortimer Road

90

Lodge Farm

2

Thrift Wood

Tom

Tit Lane

Bryant's Lane

3

05

A414 CHELMSFORD ROAD

Little Meadows

Conduit Lane

Post Office Road

Rectory Lane

4

Tyndales

SOUTHEND ROAD

Nursery Farm

Hill Farm

Woodham Mortimer

Hyde Woods

BURNHAM

ROAD

5

204

Hyde Chase

E F 55 G Little Grange H

81 82

B1010

Hazeleigh

Works

A Nathan's Lane

B

40

C

D

5 66

04

67

Margaretting Road

Southwood
Farm

I

King
Wood

2

Writtle Road

Coptfold
Hall

03

Golf Course

3

Hyla
Golf

ess

Bearman's
Farm

J15

4

A12

Wh

02

Ivy Barns Lane

Wantz

Margaretting

J14

dley
een

5

Penny's Lane

Road

Orton Close

Maldon Rd

Jennings Pl

B1002

Peacocks

Coptage La

Margaretting
CE Primary
School

A 5 66

B

67

C

D

Hylands House
& Park

Elm
Farm

41

E F G H

69 70 04

I

LONDON

Centenary Circle

HILL

MILE

THREE

Butts Way

Goat Hall Lane

Horse And Groom Lane

2

Ru
Ma

03

Bekeswell Lane

Mill Hill

P

3

Margaret

Co
Bui

50

River Wid

Lodge Farm

Margaretting Road

Wood Farm

4

Whitesbridge Lane

Durrant's
Farm

A12

Swan Lane

202

5

A12

Crondon
Hall

69 70

E F G H

Molehill
Common

Mitn Rd
Vica
Park Wrcs Ct
View C
Corner
Close
West Hanningfield
F
The Westerlings
Heycroft Way
43
G
Pontlands
Park Country
Hotel
The Grove

73

H
The Grove
74

SOUTHEND ROAD
A1

04

Lawn
Cemetery

Centenary Circle

I

West Hanningfield Road

J17

2

Vicarage Lane

Centenary Circle

Great
Mascalls

03

Brook Farm

Centenary Circle

A12

3

Brook Lane

Little and Great Sir Hughes Lane

52

Little
Sir Hughes

**Baddow
Park**

**Little
Mascalls**

4

Great
Sir Hughes

A130

West Hanningfield Road

202

Peveril
Hall

5

E   **F**   **G**   **H**
73   74

Tanfield
Tye